More Than a Conqueror

Achieving Personal Fulfillment

in Government Service

2nd edition

Daryl D. Green, MA
Estraletta A. Green, PMP, REM

More Than a Conqueror

Achieving Personal Fulfillment
in Government Service

2nd edition

Daryl D. Green, MA
Estraletta A. Green, PMP, REM

All Rights Reserved. Copyright © 2014 by Daryl Green

All rights reserved. Except as permitted under the Copyright Act of 1976, no part of this publication may be reproduced or distributed in any form or by any means, electronic or mechanical, including photocopying and recording, or stored on any information storage or retrieval system, without the written permission of the publisher.

Although the authors and publisher have exhaustively researched all sources to ensure the accuracy and completeness of the information contained in this book, we assume no responsibility for errors, inaccuracies, omissions, or any inconsistency herein. Anything appearing derogatory to people or organizations is unintentional. Readers should use their own judgment or an attorney or other experts for their individual concerns.

For information on ordering in bulk, please contact:

PMLA
P.O. Box 32733
Knoxville, TN 37930-2733
(865)602-7702
advice@darylgreen.org
www.darylgreen.org

Dedication

This hook is a tribute to all of the faithful, hardworking government employees (past and present) who have given their talents to the betterment of society. We also pay tribute to all of the pioneers who came before us and allowed us to grow in their footsteps. It is with all sincerity that we acknowledge these people.

Conquerors:

"..in all these things we are more

than conquerors..."

Romans 8:37

Contents

Acknowledgements 13

Preface 15

Introduction 19

Government Life Is Changing 27

Create a Vision: Seeing Beyond Tomorrow 35

Market Your Skills 41

Celebrate That Volunteer Spirit 51

Conclusion 63

About the Authors 67

References 73

Recommended Readings / Noted Resources 75

Appendices 79

Additional Government Knowledge- Appendix A .. 81

Transitioning Government Skills to a Home-based Business - Appendix B 85

Sample of a Personal Action Plan - Appendix C 87

Determine Your Volunteer Spirit - Appendix D 91

Determine Your Potential for Starting a Small Business - Appendix E 93

Other Books by Dr. Green 95

Acknowledgements

We wish to take this opportunity first to thank God for guiding our footsteps and giving His son, Jesus, to our world. We want to thank our immediate family— our children Mario, Sharlita, and Demetrius. You continue to supply us with plenty of love. God has blessed us with government advisors who have guided our careers. We want to thank our mothers, Mrs. Lucy Andrews and Annette Green Elias for providing us with ample advice. We want to also thank Rudy Cruz and Santos Ortega for recruiting us into government service and giving us a great start on life. You need good people in order to produce a special project. The following individuals provided extraordinary help in completing this project: Tina Pooler, Carol Ross, Sharon Partin, and Dationa Carter.

We want to also thank the librarians, especially the Knoxville Public Library for their assistance in our research. We want to thank everyone who read, evaluated, and commented on our book because your feedback was critical in our success. Lastly, we want to thank our many neighbors and friends who gave us tremendous support. There are too many to mention. We want to thank the Shreveport community, the Mobile community, the Tri-Cities community in Washington (where we started our government service), and the Knoxville\Oak Ridge area. We understand our accomplishments were not made alone. May God continue to bless your journey.

Preface

Many people don't understand the drum that my wife Estraletta and I march to. Why should anybody be concerned about employment in a stable, government environment? Our world changed. In 1996, a reduction in force (RIF) threatened our office. Estraletta and I found ourselves close to the bottom of a retention list. At that particular time, my wife and I were both senior engineers in the government sector. A sense of hopelessness encompassed our office. Many felt that without a government job the world was going to end. We, however, realized that we didn't need to worry about any downsizing. Through the years, we had acquired some very remarkable skills and experiences. The only question was, how were we going to market those skills? By using our management expertise, we formed a consulting firm. (We found, however, that many of our co-workers were content after the RIP scare was over.) The lesson we learned was to sharpen our skills and never let someone else decide our career path. Don't get too comfortable in your job. Have you ever had a manager who didn't care about his people? How did you feel? It is also apparent that few managers are concerned about employee career development. Where is the mentoring? We caution you not to get too comfortable in your jobs while the rest of the nation is going through unprecedented change. Where much is given, much is required is a testimony to our desire to live a fulfilled life. Government service is a noble undertaking because civilians give to the betterment of society. It's a shame that most people don't value this sacrifice— even within the government. Unfortunately, too many managers and organizations do not value the importance of their employees. These managers are great at developing goals and distributing tasks, but are unsuccessful at motivating and inspiring their workforce. Should there be

Preface

any surprise when outstanding employees leave a bad situation? For example, many young people come into government service with lots of energy but soon lose hope because they are overcome by negativism. F or many outstanding staff, government life can be a little discouraging if you don't know how the system operates. We understand that God has a special calling for each of us. If we fail to reach our potential in life, we are not just failing ourselves, we are failing God. People approach us routinely and ask how we can do all of these things (writing, talk shows, public speaking, teaching, etc.). It takes a great deal of managing and a clear understanding of what we enjoy. We hear people talking about what they plan to do when they retire. Retirement means happiness will begin for them. Actually, what they are saying is they are going to wait to finally become happy. Why wait? There is no guarantee that you'll make it to retirement. *More Than a Conqueror* is a positive message about how a whole nation of government employees can find liberation among the politics and red tape. The purpose of this book is to provide hope in the midst of this uncertainty. We hope that you can visualize your own silver lining. With a new sense of direction, we hope you will be able to reenergize yourself and showcase a better you. Now is the perfect time to start.

1

Introduction

"If a man does not keep pace with his companions, perhaps it is because lie hears a different drummer. Let him step to the music which he hears, however measured or far away."

Henry David Thoreau

I came to my office. I thought it was going to be a normal day at my government desk. It wasn't. One of the managers had resigned. I was totally left in disbelief. Mr. CM (we use only his initials for our point) was bright, young, and a visionary despite working in a bureaucracy. He was known for his coalition building and networking abilities. Although he was one of the youngest managers in our office, I felt his path to senior ranks was certain. Yet, he opted to leave the safety net of government life to start his own consulting business. I later interviewed him on our talk show and asked why he left. Mr.CM said he had reached a point in his life where he wanted more. More? The search for greater fulfillment is a confusing process to many people who can only see the current moment. How can you desire more when you are comfortable in your position and status? Through the years, I have seen more people leave government service for a different purpose in life. I find this passion refreshing when you consider all of the risks involved; however, I do feel everyone has to find his/her own path toward self-fulfillment. One shoe doesn't fit everybody. Yes, there is more to life than just salary and security (although these are very valuable during downsizing). Some people working in government organizations feel bitter and angry because they don't have a life outside of their job. Don't be that person!

Government service is a key institution in our society. President John Kennedy challenged the science community

Introduction

to send a man to the moon. The United States made a commitment to create the first atomic bomb. These historical events were all driven by the government sector. Within the government are some of the most creative people in the world.

Some people working in government organizations feel bitter and angry because they don't have a life outside of their job.

In today's environment, competition among American companies is fierce as they compete with other international businesses. Sadly, most organizations continue to make the mistake of investing heavily in technology and operations instead of developing their people. Some career opportunities, which government employees receive, are far better than those Fortune 500 companies can provide.

Government employees already have special skills. The key is to learn how to make those skills profitable. Many skills have great application outside the bureaucratic community.

Today, many employees are being impacted by the realities of global competition, and the government has no exemption. According to one government study, Americans hold many different jobs by the time they reach their thirties. Many companies feel that they must reorganize to stay competitive in the world market. Individuals are faced with decisions that center on professional ethics, loyalty, and career development. What can employees do to develop their careers during this time of uncertainty in employment? First, they must maximize their work effectiveness and maintain their competitive advantage. Highly energized workers should be proactive and take the following actions: (a) assess their talents; (b) identify career goals and develop realistic career plans; and (c) improve their chances for specific target positions by obtaining the necessary training and experience. In today's climate, failure to recognize opportunities is a potentially fatal mistake.

I urge you to take personal responsibility for learning new skills and new ways of doing business. Like many people in advanced technical fields, it is important for government employees to keep up with the most current, state-of-the-art techniques. Employees can take advantage of a broad range of training and development activities through their organizations. Assignments can be used to expand skills, apply existing skills to new challenges, and help limit over-dependence on a single manager or mentor. This book is designed to focus on achieving a more fulfilled government life at the federal level; however, it is also applicable to most employees in the government sector, whether at the local, county/parish, or state level. Although this book is slanted toward government life, other individuals with a desire to achieve more will also find benefit in this reading.

We have spent many years studying personal development. Our second book, *Awakening the Talents Within* (see figure), was written to help individuals gain control of their lives. We hope to give you this same liberating feeling in the arena of government service. We hope to challenge you to look beyond your pay grade and what your supervisor gives you on your performance appraisal. You are now ready to take this voyage to enlightenment and self-determination. Enter with care!

Introduction

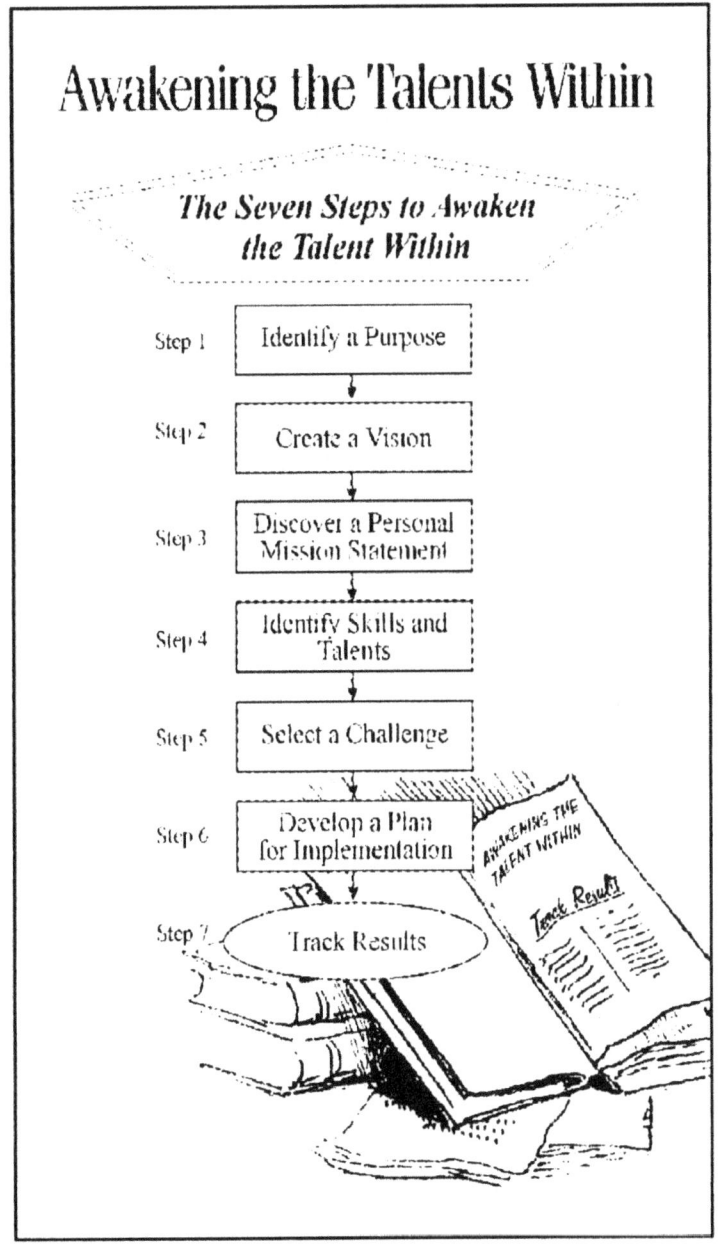

2

Government Life Is Changing

"Any man who selects a goal in life which can be fully achieved has already defined his own limitation"

Cavett Robert

Government employees should not relax during this time of enormous change. You cannot afford to think you are just going to get your 2 5-year pin and happily retire. It is also a fatal mistake to believe you have absolute security. America spent most of the 80s and 9 0 s listening to politicians promise a much smaller government. Some workers within the structure resisted the changes and went along with business as usual, hoping this mandate would go away. It didn't. At the end of fiscal year (FY) 1996, federal employment was approximately 1.94 million. Even a giant organization like the federal government is impacted by today's environment and is in the midst of downsizing its organizations. The federal government is well behind private industry in implementing restructuring. After the September 11th terrorist attacks on America, the economic slowdown has impacted both businesses and the nonprofit sector. People are losing jobs and are forced to change their priorities and lifestyles. Government employment is no exception.

Federal employees are undergoing some unparalleled changes. President Bush and his administration are now left to decide the future of the government structure. Initially in his presidency, Bush sought to eliminate 40,000 managers in the federal sector in the mid-level and senior management chain. He also hoped to transfer at least 425,000 jobs to the private sector. Squeezing the government workforce is nothing new. Former president Bill Clinton also made this an action item during his administration. After his inauguration, Clinton issued an Executive Order for agencies to cut 1 00,000 federal jobs over the next three years. As a result, the federal workforce has been downsized to its lowest level in more than 3 0 years. In former vice president Al Gore's National Performance Review in September 1993, he called on agencies to make management reforms to eliminate 252,000 positions over five years, which included the 100,000 positions called for in the Executive Order. Workforce reductions were targeted at management control positions that added little value to taxpayers' services.

Federal employees are undergoing some unparalleled changes.

Many of the non-Defense agencies have used buy-outs to encourage people to leave the federal payroll. In 2002, President Bush issued the President Agenda to improve federal government performance. He stated we must have a government that thinks differently, so we need to recruit talented and imaginative people to public service. This philosophy has provided a shock to the civilian workforce. Employees are now concerned about the A-76 Competitions because of the potential for lost jobs. A-76 refers to the Office of Management and Budget (OMB) Circular A-76 (Performance of Commercial Activities) that requires government agencies to determine if their work functions can be performed by the private sector cheaper and better. This A-76 Competition will continue to be a distraction to most federal employees and could create more personnel issues in the future.

Why would anyone want to change the government? Well, the government suffers from a bad public image. The

Government Life Is Changing

end of the Cold War was one indicator of the decline in government service. Federal workers are faced with making major decisions. According to a survey conducted for the government, 74 percent of government executives surveyed said that federal workforce quality was declining or staying the same. Public opinion is poor about government workers. Between FY 1993 and 1996, Defense civilians accounted for about 64 percent of the workforce reduction. Older employees must now decide if it's worth retiring early and taking the buyout or waiting it out for better times. According to US News & World Report in 2002, there will be huge experience gaps. With 53 percent of federal employees qualifying for retirement within five years, as many as 954,000 jobs could be vacant. This is what many within the establishment call Brain Drain. The Government will lose most of its experienced people in the upcoming years with little hope of replacement. Because of the Office of Personnel Management (OPM) regulations on Reduction in Force, the

Government could also lose its highly skilled, younger workforce.

There have been numerous studies about the danger of losing talented people. The Government Accountability Office (GAO) released a report called Human Capital: Managing Human Capital in the 21st Century. The GAO study explained that agencies damaged their mission when they reduced the influx of new talented employees due to budget constraints. In the past few years, more than 100,000 employees aged 35 and under have left the federal workforce, and the hiring of younger workers has decreased from a high of 70,000 in the late 80s to less than 10,000 in 1994. Although government employment was once thought of as a secure job, government reforms have changed the way younger employees see it. Typically in a downsizing situation, younger employees are most vulnerable to layoffs because they generally have the least seniority. According to one study, younger people today are more attracted to small business careers and have a low opinion of large institutions in both the public and the private sectors. Younger employees are more prone to make career changes. The students who are future employees see the worst in government life in the midst of scandals and corruption. Budget cuts have slowed down promotions and special government programs that once helped younger Employees develop their careers. All of these things contribute to the uncertainty of federal service.

Profile of Federal Civilian

Non-Postal Employee

Demographics

Age: 45.2 years for full-time permanent employee

Length of Service: 16.3 years

Educational Level: 39.8% bachelor's degree or higher

Gender: 55.8% men, 44.2% women

Race: 29.4% minority group

Disability: 7.2%

Veterans: 25.2%

Job Characteristics

Average Full-Time Annual Base Salary: $43,319
(adjusted to locality pay)

General Schedule (GS) Grade: 9average

Tenure: 90% permanent appointments

Occupation and PATCO: 86% White Collar, 14% Blue Collar

Pay System: 73% GS, 14% wage system and 13% others

Total in this Profit: 1,836,052 of which 1,607,814 are full-time permanent

Source: U.S. Office of Personnel Management's Central Personnel Data File (September 1997)

Create a Vision: Seeing Beyond Tomorrow

"The time is always right to do what is right"

Martin Luther King, Jr.

Do you expect to live the same old way this year? Have you set New Year's resolutions in the past and failed? Some people feel like they are caught in a bad dream. You don't need to feel that way. People who achieve great things maintain a positive outlook about themselves. They paint mental pictures of their victories. Dreams do come true if you believe. When I write books, I can see the end of what I am writing. I can visualize the light at the end of the tunnel. If you can harness the power of your imagination, your future will be brighter.

Have you ever watched Michael Jordan close his eyes and shoot a free throw? Have you thought about how Julia Roberts can play so realistic a role in a movie? Creating visual images is the key. Mental visualization is all about your ability to maximize your imagination and operate on faith. It's not just for the rich, highly educated, and powerful; visualization is done in all walks of life-doctors, teachers, actors, public speakers, and other occupations. This is not something you just pick up, however. You need to practice. High achievers use their imagination to prepare their performance. When you mentally rehearse, you visualize the desired outcome. How can you use this concept in your life? Mental visualization can only work if you believe in yourself. Belief is a major component. The Law of Beliefs states you act and respond according to the images you create in your mind. You must believe you are capable of achieving your vision. Your internal belief system impacts how you deal with circumstances. Maxwell Maltz, author of *Psycho-Cybernetics,* states, Positive thinking cannot be used effectively as a patch or a crutch to the same self image.

Mental visualization can only work if you believe in yourself.

In fact, it is literally impossible to really think about a particular situation, as long as you hold a negative concept of self. Your self-concept can haunt you because you keep generating self-limiting beliefs about your abilities. That's why creating a vision takes building yourself from the inside out and not the outside in. You must start creating a reality for your dreams (perhaps something your family and friends will not understand). Here are some steps to follow in building your vision:

1. Set aside a quiet place for your mental visualization.

2. Determine your desired outcome.

3. Imagine yourself in the specific situation (cool, calm, and relaxed).

4. Run yourself mentally through the situation or event.

5. Use visualization in conjunction with hard work and knowledge.

6. Repeat mental visualization until your goal is reached.

Mental visualization can be a powerful tool if you use it. Success begins in the mind. When you build your mental strength, you will be able to increase your future opportunities. High performers routinely use mental rehearsal to help them obtain success. Nathaniel Brandon, author of *The Power of Self-Esteem,* says, If we do have realistic confidence in our mind and value, if we feel secure within ourselves, we tend to experience the world as open to us and to respond appropriately to challenges and opportunities.

Do you have the ability to see beyond your current situation? A good attitude provides a great launching pad for your dreams. Start today and wake up to achieving your dreams.

4

Market Your Skills

The future belongs to those who believe in the beauty of their dreams.

Eleanor Roosevelt

Federal employees are some of the brightest and most innovative people in the country (including accountants, astronauts, scientists, business professionals, administrative professionals, engineers, and a host of other disciplines). However, the general public's perception is that government employees are lazy, bureaucratic, non-caring, and out-of-touch with the average American. Nevertheless, the talent is there-hidden behind the red tape and bureaucracy. For example, the Department of Energy (DOE) has multiple missions that include energy technology, research and development, national security, environmental quality, and expanding the frontiers of scientific knowledge. DOE has funded research that has led to 71 Nobel Prizes. The scientific and technological talents of the 17,000 federal employees and 106,000 contractor employees have enabled advances in such areas as energy efficiency processes, new medical diagnostic tools, new environmental technology, and special security systems, to name a few. Many federal employees' duties are similar to those in private business. A correlation can be made that shows how government skills can be translated into the private sector (see Appendix B).

God has equipped people with many skills; unfortunately, many never truly tap this deep reservoir.

You need to take a personal assessment of yourself. These are times to make you lose your mind— layoffs, acquisitions and mergers, and an unstable global economy. According to one study, today's workers will change careers at least three times in their lives. Through many years of working, you have gained extensive experience and knowledge. God has equipped people with many skills; unfortunately, many never truly tap this deep reservoir. You need to be candid and honest about your marketability. Do you consider your job challenging? Do you like working by yourself? Can you speak more than one language? You need to identify the skills you currently have and what you enjoy doing. It will not be easy; however, bookstores and libraries have many personal assessment tools you can use.

Take responsibility for learning new skills and new ways of doing business. In every occupation, making difficult decisions under pressure is a sign of leadership. In customer-driven companies, the ability to make decisions at all levels in an organization is an emerging priority and enables these corporations to respond more rapidly to opportunities to upgrade quality and capture new advantages in the marketplace. Find ways to improve and enhance your abilities. Develop your own personal action plan as a guiding light for your career (see Appendix C). You can also contact your local college to meet with a career counselor or talk to someone at an employment agency. These are all free. Skills developed in government work are transferable skills that you can use to get another job or start your own business. The key to making this change is not necessarily to master a new skill, but to realign your old skills to meet the changing business environment and future challenges. Many studies reveal that you will perform better when you do what you enjoy.

Steps To Transfer Your Skills

1. Take a personal assessment of skills.

2. Focus on your goals.

3. Develop a personal action plan.

4. Determine what resources you need.

5. Review and update your plan routinely.

Determine Your Transferable Skills

Personal Assessment Exercise

Directions: The purpose of this exercise is to familiarize you with the transferable skills that are hidden within you. Many of the skills can be categorized as people, data, and things. Some skills can be rather simple, while others can be very complex. The skills should be ranked as follows: L = low, M = medium or H = high. Low means you have the skill, but you don't enjoy it. Medium means you have the skill, but you feel indifferent about it. High means you have the skill, and you enjoy it. List where you have demonstrated the skill (job, special assignment, church, home, hobby, community, etc.). Please feel free to make copies for completion.

Type I: People Skills		
Skill	**Place Used**	**Rank (L-M-H)**
Advising/Consulting		
Administration		
Assisting		
Coordinating		
Coaching		
Communicating		
Listening		
Supervising		
Scheduling		
Teaching		
Handling Conflict		
Selling		
Motivating		
Others		

Type II: Data Skills		
Skill	Place Used	Rank (L-M-H)
Analyzing		
Computing		
Evaluating		
Strategizing		
Reasoning		
Coordinating Data		
Writing		
Editing		
Compiling Information		
Identifying Key Points		
Critiquing		
Others		

Market Your Skills

Type III: Thing Skills		
Skill	**Place Used**	**Rank (L-M-H)**
Assembling		
Graphic Designing		
Drawing		
Building		
Fixing		
Organizing		
Operating Machine Equipment		
Computer Programming		
Developing		
Creating		
Inventing		
Typing		
Others		

Action Steps for Implementation

a) List your high and medium skills.

b) Concentrate on your high and medium skills because these may be your Center of Excellence (where you can make the most improvements).

c) Brainstorm some potential small business ventures.

d) Consider applying your talents in another industry or application.

e) Conduct research and develop a plan.

5

Celebrate That Volunteer Spirit

When the best leader's work is done the people say, We did it ourselves.

Lao Tzu

As America watched the devastation of Hurricane Katrina in 2005, many people were horrified at the living conditions of the victims. As the government tried to assess the situation, citizens from around the country were being mobilized to help those in need. One of our friends was so disgusted with the situation in New Orleans that he took his own personal time and went down to help the people in the Gulf coast area. We would say lie was not the exception but the rule. Many people felt a warm feeling inside because they had given of themselves. There is something special about giving to others that no scientific formula can explain. Many people with special skills in the government provide critical leadership to various civic and social organizations in their communities. Ironically, these same people may hate their government job because they are not valued for their talents. For example, a government office manager may work in an environment where she is not respected or valued because of her pay grade. She is never given special assignments or career development activities. She soon grows tired of asking to be treated fairly and becomes a robot in her job. This is a tragic situation because this office manager is special. In her private life, she serves as the chairperson for her local nonprofit organization and is highly respected in her community because of her leadership abilities. Unfortunately, I have seen some talented people in the government go underutilized. How in the world could this happen in the government? Through our government experiences and meeting hundreds of people in our seminars, we clearly notice several issues related to the government's human capital issues.

Sadly, many talented employees simply grow tired of these low expectations and give the organization what it wants, no more and no less.

First, one of the problems is that most government managers do not understand how to evaluate talent or how to develop it. Secondly, most managers do not love their employees. What do you mean about loving employees? These leaders do not value their employees on a very personal level. Of course these managers are not mean folks, but they do not have a personal interest in the development of their employees— making sure those employees get what they want out of life and out of their job. This is a shame because the government's investment is lost. Max DePree, author of *Leadership is an Art,* views leaders as corporate liberators, bringing out the best in their followers. DePree explains. The measure of leadership is not the quality of the head, but the tone of the body. The signs of outstanding leadership appear primarily among the followers. Are the followers reaching their potential? Sadly, many talented employees simply grow tired of these low expectations and give the organization what it wants, no more and no less.

One great option for using your underutilized skills is to volunteer. You can do volunteer work and accept new responsibilities. You can even start your own nonprofit organization to address a need within your community. Take a look at your community. There are numerous organizations that can use your skills and your leadership. How do you get involved? Talk to co-workers, family, and friends. Check the local newspapers. Contact your public library. There are as many causes as there are spam emails on your computer. Don't, however, settle for just any volunteering assignment. We have seen that doing too much or doing the wrong thing burns out many people. You do not have to volunteer just because you are requested to do so. Think about it first. You need to determine what cause(s) you are willing to give your time and energy to (See Appendix D). What are you passionate about? Use your volunteering assignment as a way to learn new skills, build your networking base, and stimulate new friendships. Your volunteer spirit will help revitalize your energy in doing that mundane government job. You will find a new sense of purpose. In the meantime, I hope that government managers become more people-focused, thereby stimulating the personal growth of their employees. Get that volunteer spirit today!

Celebrate an Entrepreneur's Life

I will prepare, and some day my chance will come.

Abraham Lincoln

Business ownership can refresh your abilities. There are so many ways you can build your skills and maintain a high level of purpose. You can change jobs and accept a new assignment; however, there is no greater feeling than using your abilities in the private sector. You are taking on the title of entrepreneur. Maybe you don't think you have the courage to do it— to become your own boss. We are not talking about losing your life's earnings in your pension or Thrift Savings Plan. I'm talking about a part-time or weekend venture that allows you to use your special talents (it's like an insurance package against your organization's leaving you high and dry). About 80 percent of your success will depend on your ability to understand your customers' needs.

The most compelling attraction to using your skills outside of work is to accomplish something meaningful—without the hassle of any red tape. Can you handle this competitive environment that rewards success based on merit? I feel this situation will help you keep the hunger instinct so that you don't get complacent in your government job. You get a fresh energy boost to your career while accepting new challenges. First, you need to evaluate what type of things you enjoy. People who are successful in their field generally enjoy what they are doing. Is there a hobby you can turn into income? Once you decide on your idea, you need to develop a plan. Determine your needs. How much training do you need? How much money? Who can help you? Learn everything you possibly can about your new business. Find individuals who are working in that area and talk with them. You may have to develop new skills to reach your dreams. You may have to go back to school (if only for a short period).

About 80 percent of your success will depend on your ability to understand your customers' needs.

Home-based businesses are the biggest billion-dollar industry in America. Some of these businesses are the sole source of income, while others are not. The best time to discover your interest in a business is while you still have a job so that you can minimize the risk to your financial security. This second job can relate to what you do at work, which will increase your on-the-job career flexibility, while helping you develop additional skills. You can also test one of your hobbies and see if it has the potential to be more. You should check with your legal or ethics organization to make sure there's no problem with your outside venture. Set realistic goals. You have to be self-motivated. You won't have a boss holding your promotion as a threat. You have to have heart!

How do you find the money? Many people fund their small businesses with personal savings and by borrowing from relatives or friends. Still others use credit cards or take out bank loans. No question about it, you will need capital to succeed. The amounts will vary according to your product/service and your personal goals. Most new businesses have some cash flow problems. You can begin with very little money, depending on your business venture. Try to find a business that focuses on your strengths and maximizes your abilities (See Appendix E). The Internet is a new frontier for people with creativity and guts. More than $100 billion worth of transactions have been conducted on the Net. These business communities are made of electronic networks of distributors, suppliers, customers, and other Net-savvy businesses.

Conclusion

Great spirits have always encountered violent opposition from mediocre minds.

Albert Einstein

The American workplace is likely to remain in a state of continual chaos as organizations focus on restructuring and seeking greater efficiencies. Federal workers are in a similar condition and must face the reality of moving on rather than retiring from federal service. These uncertainties of life will continue to test the motivation of employees in performing their jobs. Federal workers need to continuously observe the early warning signals of problems at work, which are often so subtle that they are mistaken for non work-related stress.

It is vital to recognize early feelings of discomfort and appropriately attach them to the workplace. No one wants to admit his/her job is in jeopardy. Most people will experience a predictable sequence of reactions during work changes (restructuring, reorganizations, etc.). Employees should first develop special skills to help correctly interpret the early warning signs of change within an organization and their personal lives.

These uncertainties of life will continue to test the motivation of employees in performing their jobs.

Getting caught off guard can happen for many reasons. Most people communicate indirectly, especially if the message is uncomfortable or negative. And although people and institutions may say what they really mean, they rarely say it directly. Career transition will provide a great challenge for future workers. The way government

Conclusion

employees deal with these critical times will govern whether they stay on track in achieving their goals or suffer failure. Time is short. However, there is no need to despair. The future is bright for employees with a more than a conqueror attitude about life. Celebrate your life today and have a more fulfilled life!

About the Authors

Daryl and Estraletta Green are one of the leading authorities for GenXers on helping working families get more control of their lives. They are former nationally syndicated columnists who  have been noted and quoted in such sources as *Associate Press, USA Today, BET,* and *Ebony Magazine.*

Daryl D. Green, who works for the Department of Energy (DOE), is a Louisiana native. He is also the author of several books, *Awakening the Talents Within* and *My Cup Runneth Over: Setting Goals for Single Parents and Working Couples.* One Tennessee newspaper called him a 20st Century Renaissance man. He is a manager, engineer, TV talk show host, poet, and professor. He received the DOE Community Service Award and the Pasco Martin Luther King, Jr. Humanitarian Award for this effort. Daryl is also listed in *Who's Who in U.S. Writers, Editors & Poets; Who's Who Among International Professionals;* and *Who's Who Among Top Executives and Successful Businesses.* He is the past president of the Clinch River Club of Toastmasters, International, and the Oak Ridge Chapter of Blacks in Government (BIG). Daryl received a BS in Mechanical Engineering at Southern University A & M and an MA in Organizational. Management at Tusculum College, and is currently a doctoral student at Regent University. He is involved with numerous programs and projects to better assist the human spirit.

Estraletta A. Green is a native of Mobile, Alabama. Estraletta received a BS in Civil Engineering from Southern University A & M and is a lifetime learner. She has worked for DOE as a team leader and strategic planner for the Environmental Management program. She is also certified as a Registered Environmental Manager and Project Management Professional. Estraletta's accomplishments are

About the Authors

many. She was featured in *Black Collegian* as an Outstanding Black Female Engineer and listed in *Who's Who Among International Professionals*. Estraletta was selected as a delegate to the Management Institute for Professional Women hosted by Washington State University. She is very active in her community and is a former BIG officer in Tennessee. Estraletta has served as Federally Employed Women's Program Manager, past president of Toastmasters International, church trustee member, and vice president for Delta Sigma Theta, Incorporated, to name a few.

PMLA Company

Daryl & Estraletta Green, Owners

Daryl and Estraletta Green founded Performance Management & Logistics Associates (PMLA) in January of 1997. They knew that much was expected of them in the business world because of their many skills and experiences. All of their lives they have worked on events and activities together at work and in the community. Now, they use their engineering and management backgrounds to help people make good decisions. Their services include professional speaking, personal advisement, seminars, new business start-up consulting, small business marketing, self-publishing advisement, and family management. The Greens also support an array of community and service programs that benefit children and families.

If you would like them to speak to your organization or would like more information about their company services, please contact them:

About the Authors

PMLA

P.O. Box 32733

Knoxville, TN 37930-2733

Phone: (865)602-7858

Email: advice@darylgreen.org

Homepage: www.darylgreen.org

References

Bock, Walter H. and Jeff Senne, *CyberPower for Business,* Career Press, 1996.

Bolles, Richard, *What Color Is Your Parachute,* The Ten Press, 1994.

Brown, Les, *The Courage to Live Your Dreams,* HarperAudio, 1993, Publishing, 1998.

DePree, Max, *Leadership is an Art,* A Dell Trade Paperback, 1989.

Frankl, Viktor E., *Man's Search for Meaning,* Washington Square Press, 1984.

Green, Daryl D., *Awakening the Talents Within,* The Writers Club Press, 2000.

Green, Daryl D., My Cup Runneth Over: Setting Goals for Single Parents and Working Couples, Triangle Publications, 1998.

Hill, Napoleon, *Think and Grow Rich,* Ballantine Books, 1988.

Kimbro, Dennis, *What Makes the Great Great*, DoubleDav Publications, 1995.

McGinnis, Alan, The Balanced Life: Achieving Success in Work and Love, Augsburg, 1997.

Morley, Patrick, *The Rest of Your Life*, Zondervan Publishing, 1998.

Naisbitt, John and Patricia Aburdene, *Megatrends 2000,* Avon Books, 1990.

Pinskey, Raleigh, *101 Ways to Promote Yourself,* Avon Books, 1997.

Popcorn, Faith, *Clicking,* HarperCollins Publishers, 1996.

Sinetar, Marsha, Do What You Love, the Money Will Follow, Dell Books, 1989.

Wilson, Susan B., *Goal Setting,* American Management Association, 1994.

Recommended Readings / Noted Resources

Learn about information designed to assist small businesses in competing on a global front. Contact the organizations for current information.

BOOKS/DOCUMENTS

Internet

The Complete Small Business Internet Guide by Tom & Lori Heatherington

Internet World by Cliff Allen

Essential Business Tactics for the Net by Larry Chase & Eileen Shulock

101 Ways to Promote Your Web Site by Susan Sweeney

B2B by Michael J. Cunningham

Net Gain by John Hagell III

Net Worth by John Hagell III

Global Market

Growing Your Business Globally by Robert Taft

Marketing Resources

Knock Your Socks Off by Jay Conrad Levinson

The Leadership Challenge James Kouzes and Barry Posner

Guerrilla Marketing by Jay Conrad Levinson

Relationship Marketing Regis McKenna

Strategic Thinking

The Portable MBA in Entrepreneurship by William Bygrave and Andrew Zacharakis

Growing Your Business Globally by Robert Taft

Strategic Thinking Rex C. Mitchell, Ph.D. (paper, 2005)

Small Business Enterprises/Home-based Businesses

The Best Home Business for the 21st Century by Sarah & Paul Edward

Four Steps to Building a Profitable Business by Deborah Brown-Volkman

The Entrepreneur Guide by D. Brown

Recommended Readings / Noted Resources

Going Part-time by Cindy Tolliver & Nancy Chambers

How to Start a Home-Based Writing Business by Lucy Parker

WEBSITES FOR SMALL BUSINESS ENTERPRISES

Business Assistance

Small Business Administration www.sba.gov

Internal Revenue Service www.irs.gov

SCORE www.score.org

Fortune Small Business www.fortunesb.com

Business Planning Resource www.bplans.com

Smart Business www.smartbiz.com

Working Solo www.workingsolo.com

Home Business Research www.homebusinessresearch.com

Entrepreneur www.entrepreneur.com

Appendices

Additional Government Knowledge — Appendix A

Government Skills to Home-based Business Transition - Appendix B

Personal Action Plan - Appendix C

Personal Cause Assessment – Appendix D

The Entrepreneur Assessment – Appendix E

Appendix A

Additional Government Knowledge

Learn about government programs that personnel didn't want you to know about, and career opportunities that your supervisor didn't want you to ask him about. Contact the organizations for current information.

The Government Affairs Institute at Georgetown University

The Capital Hill Fellowship Program provides Executive Branch personnel the opportunity to serve in assignments in the Legislative Branch for 7 or 12 months. Fellows receive training and experience on Capital Hill. The Catalog of Courses can be obtained at http://gai.georgetown.edu/.

U.S. Department of Agriculture

Aspiring Leader Program is a 6-month, part-time career development program that is designed to provide a foundation of team leadership training and experience. It is open to full-time federal employees (GS-5, GS-6, or GS-7) who demonstrate potential leadership qualities and abilities.

The Women's Executive Leadership Program is a 1-year, part-time career development program that is designed to provide a foundation of management training and appropriate developmental experiences to high potential GS-11/12 level individuals in preparation for higher-level management or executive positions.

The Executive Potential Program is a 1-year, part-time career development program that is designed to provide a foundation of management training and appropriate developmental experiences to high potential GS/GM-13/14 level individuals in preparation for higher-level management or executive positions.

Appendix A

This information can be obtained at http://www.grad.usda.gov/.

Training Towards a Degree or Certification

The federal government will not pay for an employee to receive a degree. However, each agency may fund individual courses that relate to the agency mission. If, by taking individual courses, an employee receives a degree, the degree is an incidental by-product of the training. There is no consistency in which training is allowed and what cost will be paid (one employee was known to get a sabbatical, his salary, and a degree). The key to this process is a willing supervisor and agency support.

This information can be obtained from your training office or the Office of Personnel Management.

Mobility Assignments Between Federal and Non-Federal Offices

OPM has a special program, *InterGovernmental Personnel Act (IPA) Mobility Program,* which is part of the InterGovernmental Personnel Act of 1970. The I PA program allows federal and non-federal employees to move between public and non-profit organizations to facilitate the exchange of ideas and expertise. This is one of the biggest secrets in the government. Many people are using it; however, your current supervisor and upper management must accept the idea. New regulations are being proposed to this program that includes expanding it to include federally funded research and development centers that formerly had to apply for certification to participate. OPM no longer will require a copy of the written agreement from each IPA assignment, but will request agencies to submit an annual IPA report.

This information can be obtained from your human resource office or the Office of Personnel Management.

Appendix B

Transitioning Government Skills to a Home-based Business

Directions:

Workers must be able to market their skills. Take this time to create a short biographical sketch and use it as a marketing tool for new career opportunities. There are many opportunities to broaden your skills. The following list is only designed to get you started. Below is only a sample of possible home- based businesses making use of transferable skills:

Federal Category and Transferable Skills Possible	Possible Home-Based Business

Administrative Types: knowledge of office management

Clerk	Importer/Exporter
Office manager	Editorial Services
Secretary	Professional Organizer
	Typing Service

Business Types: knowledge of business functions

Accountant	Bookkeeper
Budget analyst	Bill-Auditing Agent
Finance specialist	Advertising Agent

Engineering/Science Types: knowledge of technical principles

Engineer	Home Inspector
Computer programmer	Shareware Developer
Technical auditor	Herb Specialist

Management Types: knowledge of management principles

Program analyst	Detective
Personnel specialist	Employee Trainer
Security specialist	Expert Service Broker
Attorney	Management Consultant

Appendix C

Sample of a Personal Action Plan
NED E. MATTHEWS
PERSONAL PLAN
2011

MISSION

The purpose of my existence is to improve the quality of life for all people by using my creative talents in the Arts.

GOALS

- To be recognized nationally for my art collection
- To produce a family well prepared for the future
- To be financially secure and wealthy
- To create a national foundation to improve the lives of black children
- To become a more spiritual-based person

SPIRITUAL GOALS

Action	Deadline	Status
Weekly family devotion	Jan 01	Ongoing
Kids participate in church activities	Jan 01	Ongoing
Attend couples' marriage conference	Sep 3-5	
Attend men's retreat	Oct 22-24	
Attend at least one Bible/prayer meeting this year	Dec	Completed
Fast, pray, and study	Jan 01	Ongoing

FINANCIAL GOALS

Action	Deadline	Status
Update financial portfolio	Dec 01	
Review credit history	Aug 31	
Look at Real Estate move	Sep 30	
Invest $5,000 in stock	Aug 19	
Secure $20 K for business through investors	Dec 19	
Video home assets	Sep 30	
Make will	Nov 02	

Appendix C

CAREER/BUSINESS GOALS

Action	Deadline	Status
Wife will change jobs	Dec 01	Completed
Become professional speaker	Dec 01	
Take online course for certification	Jan 01	

COMMUNITY GOALS

Action	Deadline	Status
Work with HBCU Awareness Day	Nov 12	Ongoing
Conduct free youth seminars	Sep 3-5	Completed
Speak at local schools	Jan 01	Completed
Support youth with financial donations	Dec 01	Completed
Speak at local churches	Jan 01	Ongoing
Write for local column for local community papers	Mar 01	Completed

PERSONAL/FAMILY GOALS

Action	Deadline	Status
Encourage kids to learn and enjoy school	Jan 01	Ongoing
Teach kids to learn to appreciate reading	Jan 01	Ongoing
Help kids with homework	Jan 01	Ongoing
Spend time with each child per week	3-5 times per week	Ongoing
Determine kids' activities for the year	Aug 01	
Plan family trips for the school year	Dec 01	
Visit a college campus	Dec 01	Completed
Attend a cultural event	Dec 01	Completed
Participate in school activities, PTA	Dec 01	

Appendix D

Determine Your Volunteer Spirit
Personal Assessment
Exercise

Answer the questions below. If you answer yes to all the questions, you are well on your way to being a servant to humanity. Feel free to copy this form to complete it.

YES   NO

____ ____ Do you enjoy helping others?

____ ____ Are you committed to seeing a project completed?

____ ____ Do you have leadership abilities, which are not being used?

____ ____ Are you passionate about a special cause? Are you willing to create a non-profit organization to satisfy this passion?

____ ____ Do you have enough energy to work a primary job and serve as a volunteer at the same time?

____ ____ Are you in good health?

____ ____ Is your family supportive of your goal to volunteer?

____ ____ Are you willing to learn new skills as a part of this volunteer effort?

Appendix E

Determine Your Potential for Starting a Small Business
Personal Assessment
Exercise

Answer the questions below. If you answer yes to all the questions, you are well on your way to becoming the captain of your own ship by starting a new business. The purpose of this exercise is to determine your interest and desire to start your own home-based business. Success is directly dependent on your ability to overcome failure and disappointment. This might not be an overnight success story. Individuals have become successful without a great deal of formal education or money; however, it is hard to succeed without the right frame of mind and commitment. Feel free to copy this form to complete it.

YES   NO

____   ____   Do you want to do more than your current job will allow you?

____   ____   Are you a self-starter?

____   ____   Are you goals-oriented?

____   ____   Are you willing to take a financial risk with possible losses?

____   ____   Do you have enough energy to work a primary and secondary job (moonlighting)?

____   ____   Are you in good health?

____   ____   Does your family support your goal of starting a business?

____   ____   Do you enjoy learning new skills?

____   ____   Are you willing to promote your business to potential customers?

Note: If you have more no's than yes's, you should reconsider becoming an entrepreneur.

Other Books by Dr. Green

Dr. Green continues to research and produce information that aims to improve society. Below is a synopsis of some of his other products:

A Call to Destiny: How to Create Effective Ways to Assist Black Boys in America provides a practical assessment of what happens to young black boys in America. It seeks to provide ways for parents, educators, and supporters to assist these boys in their positive development. Without any intervention, young black boys, regardless of their social class, will not survive in the twenty-first century. In this book, *A Call to Destiny*, you will (a) examine the severity of the problems facing young black boys, (b) learn new strategies to bring solutions to your child and the community at large, and (c) provide inspiration to continue the fight to save this generation. (**Paperback:** 50 pages, **ISBN:** 978-1442181021)

Awakening the Talents Within is a powerful, step-by-step approach that individuals can use to solve problems and enhance their overall success. This book is a wake-up call for the next generation of leaders. Dr. Green uses his charismatic style for today's hip-hop culture, dealing with a wide range of issues from stopping procrastination to creating business ownership. The solutions contained in the book reflect over ten years of managing, consulting, and teaching in government, non-profit, business, private, and academic institutions. (**Paperback**: 136 pages, **ISBN**: 978-0595146130, **Hardcover**: 140 pages, **ISBN**: 978-0595745722)

Book Publishing for Professionals provides the secrets of gaining this useful power. Packed with proven insights and advice, this book provides simple, logical steps for professionals. It includes effective writing tools, the best publishing options, and marketing strategies to make your book successful in the marketplace. It is geared toward the writer who wants to publish a non-fiction book (biography, cookbook, self-help, Christian book, textbook, etc.). (**Paperback**: 68 pages, **ISBN**: 978-1449985561, **Kindle**: 68 pages **ASIN**: B0047T7DPA, **Hardcover**: 108 pages, **ISBN**: 978-0-557-98346-9, DVD: 26 minutes, **ASIN**: B001FB4Z3G, CD: 26 minutes, **ASIN**: B004CYFBBS)

Other Books by Dr. Green

Breaking Organizational Ties provides practical strategies for employees attempting to cope in jobs or environments which they hate. While most managers are only concerned with the bottom-line, they leave their employees vulnerable to the casualties of competitive markets. This book will enable readers to (a) learn how to survive and enjoy their time at work even in a hostile environment, (b) gain greater confidence in their ability to grow while in a downsizing organization, and (c) discover the insight to go beyond their limitations by breaking the barriers of self-doubt. (**Paperback**: 124 pages, **ISBN**: 978-1450511315)

Great Customer Service: The Definitive Handbook for Today's Successful Businesses provides a framework for businesses that want sustainable success during an unstable economy. The book appeals to sales people and anyone who wants to maintain good relationships with their customers. Readers can ensure success by following the practical application of concepts outlined in the book in order to satisfy customers' needs or wants. The book addresses the topics of building a more profitable business; increasing good sustainable customer service; inspiring workers toward great organizational performance and learning how to inspire demanding customers. (Paperback: **148 pages**, ISBN: **978-1480054707**)

Don't be an Old Fool: Common Sense & Gratitude is a collection of Dr. Green's syndicated columns through the years. The book offers practical strategies for individuals who desire to make better decisions in their lives by using sound, common-sense approaches. With renewed purpose and direction, individuals will be able to energize themselves for the future. (**Paperback**: 134 pages, **ISBN**: 978- 1466236530)

Impending Danger: The Federal Handbook for Rethinking Leadership in the 21st Century provides critical answers regarding how government leaders can reduce partisan bickering by changing the current leadership paradigm. With 40 years' worth of experience in the public sector, Dr. Green and his co-author, Dr. Gary Roberts, know what they're talking about. The book provides

Other Books by Dr. Green

revelations and insights regarding political strife and the answers that can solve them. (**Hardcover:** 146 pages, **ISBN**: 978-1607971382)

More Than a Conqueror: Achieving Personal Fulfillment in Government Service is a message about how to take positive steps in achieving your goals while in government service, although any civilians will be able to benefit from this book. In *More than a Conqueror*, you will (a) go beyond your self-imposed limitations by breaking the barrier of your self-doubt and (b) protect and cultivate your life in order to bring forth the best you can in your generation. (**Paperback**: 76 pages, **ISBN**: 978-0971400887)

My Cup Runneth Over: Setting Goals for Single Parents and Working Couples guides families in setting goals for themselves. Daryl and his wife have first-hand experience on this subject, both working full-time jobs, and raising three active children. This book uses a new management process called Meshing TM. The book is very different from most family books, by focusing more on practical solutions. Dr. Green has used his and his wife's experiences as managers from government, non-profit and private business sectors to help families —regain control of their lives. Written in an informal, entertaining style, it provides information to families that gives them HOPE. Creatively illustrated with graphics and charts, the book is also indexed for quick reference. It is essential reading for families in search of purpose.

Special Awards: January Book of the Month, The Larry Young Show 1998, Special Black History Award at Atkins Library, Featured on Heaven 600 (The Top Gospel Radio Station in the Country). (**Paperback**: 108 pages, **ISBN**: 978-1889745039, **Audiobook**: 978- 1889745053, **Audio CD**: **ASIN**: B001VH787E)

Second Chance presents non-profit organizations with a way to use operations management tools for more efficiency. Non-profit organizations will become better-equipped to assist clients and constituents in meeting their needs. Dr. Green co-authored this book with one of his students. Through the eyes of student Noriko Chapman, readers will be taken on a magical journey of overcoming a difficult situation in operations management and in life. (**Paperback:** 130 pages, **ISBN:** 978-1461146070)

Selling by Objectives provides insight on how to create more sales during an economic crisis, using seven key ingredients. The book provides practical solutions that today's organizations can easily digest and implement even in an unstable economy. This book is important not only for sales people, but also for any professional involved in selling goods and services with a desire to be successful in the marketplace. Non-profit organizations, business owners, college students, professors, entrepreneurs, and other sales organizations can benefit from this book. (**Paperback***: 138 pages,* **ISBN***: 978- 1470054342)*

Writing for Professionals provides individuals with authoritative writing tools. It offers strategies, practical guidelines, resources, and a host of suggestions to help with publishing goals. The advice in this book can be useful for a wide variety of professions, including business executives, teachers, scientists, engineers, attorneys, and many others. *(***Paperback***: 240 pages,* **ISBN***: 978-1475152333)*

i

www.ingramcontent.com/pod-product-compliance
Lightning Source LLC
Chambersburg PA
CBHW051731170526
45167CB00002B/893